The Story of SKATEBOARDING

Contents

Written by Andrew Fusek Peters

The start of skateboarding

Skateboarding began in California, USA,
in the 1950s.

Surfers got bored when there were no waves.
Some of them nailed roller skate wheels to
a plank of wood.

Surfers need big waves.

Parts of a skateboard

In the 1970s, new plastic wheels were invented. They were smoother and made skating easier.

wheels

bends up at
one end

deck

trucks

5

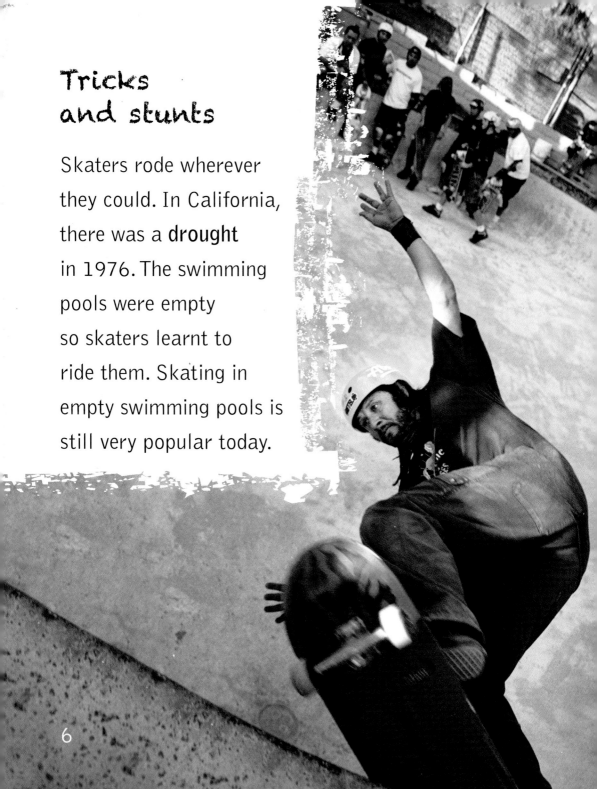

Tricks and stunts

Skaters rode wherever they could. In California, there was a **drought** in 1976. The swimming pools were empty so skaters learnt to ride them. Skating in empty swimming pools is still very popular today.

The "Ollie"

The skaters invented a trick called the "Ollie".

Bend your knees.

*Hit the back of
the board on the ground.*

*Slide your front foot to
the front of the board.*

Lift-off!

7

Some skaters wanted to do tricks on other surfaces.
A new style of skating started called "street".
Skaters used kerbs, stairs and rails to
practise tricks.

8

Ramps

Skaters began using ramps to perform **stunts**.

The "drop-in" is the most basic move on a ramp.
Skaters stand at the top to drop into the ramp.

New skateboards

Over the years, skateboards have changed even more. The wheels have become smaller and the decks have changed shape.

Skaters can now go faster and jump higher.

wheels

Protection

Skaters wear special clothes to protect themselves if they fall.

helmet

elbow pads

skate shoes

knee pads

Skateparks

Skaters travel to famous skateparks around the world to practise new tricks.

Stoke Plaza, Stoke-on-Trent, England

Lake Cunningham Regional Skatepark, California, USA

Competitions

Skateboarding is part of popular competitions such as the X Games in the USA. The best skaters from all over the world take part. It has separate street-style and **vert-ramp** competitions.

vert-ramp competition

18

street-style competition

The best skateboarders

Top riders like Tony Hawk and Shaun White have millions of fans and perform amazing stunts.

Tony Hawk on a vert ramp

Glossary

deck   the flat part of a skateboard

drought   when it hasn't rained for a long time

highest air   the distance between the skateboarder
and the nearest thing beneath them

stunt   an action that shows skill

vert ramp   a u-shaped ramp that goes from a flat wall
down to a flat bottom and then up again

Index

Tricks and stunts

the "Ollie"

the "drop-in"

vert ramp

street style

Ideas for reading

Written by Gillian Howell
Primary Literacy Consultant

Learning objectives: *(reading objectives correspond with Orange band; all other objectives correspond with Copper band)* read independently and with increasing fluency longer and less familiar texts; identify and make notes of the main points of section(s) of text; follow up others' points and show whether they agree or disagree in whole-class discussion

Interest words: skateboarding, wheels, drought, surfaces, practise, protection, famous, competitions, separate

Resources: pens, paper, ICT

Word count: 277

Getting started

- Read the title and blurb together. Ask the children to describe what they already know about skateboarding. Ask them to say what information they might learn by reading this book.

- Read the contents list together and ask the children to find the glossary and read the words and definitions together to pre-empt any difficulties.

Reading and responding

- Ask the children to read the book on their own. Remind them to use their knowledge of phonics and contextual clues to work out words they are unsure of. Prompt them to look for words within words, e.g. *kick* and *tail* are in kicktail on p4.

- Ask the children to look at the labels on p4. Ask them to say what the purpose of labelled illustrations and diagrams is.

- As they read, ask the children to find a key piece of information that they find interesting or is new to them to report back to the group later.

Returning to the book

- Turn to pp22–23 and discuss the different types of tricks and stunts that can be done on a skateboard. Which do they think would be the most exciting to watch?